The 5-Minute BIBLE STUDY MAP FOR TEEN GIRLS

A Creative Journal

Print ISBN 979-8-89151-186-6

Published by Barbour Publishing, Inc., 1810 Barbour Drive, Uhrichsville, Ohio 44683, www.barbourbooks.com

Our mission is to inspire the world with the life-changing message of the Bible.

Printed in China.

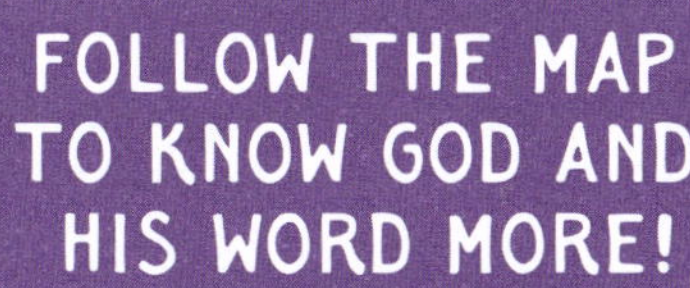

This fantastic Bible study journal provides an avenue for you to open the Bible regularly and dig in to a passage—even if you have only five minutes!

Minutes 1–2: ***Read*** carefully the scripture passage for each day's Bible study.

Minute 3: ***Understand.*** Read a brief devotional based on the day's scripture.

Minute 4: ***Apply.*** Answer the questions designed to help you apply the verses from the Bible to your own life.

Minute 5: ***Pray.*** A dedicated spot for prayer will allow you to talk to God about anything on your heart.

May *The 5-Minute Bible Study Map for Teen Girls* help you establish the discipline of studying God's Word. You will find that spending even five minutes focused on scripture and prayer has the power to make a huge difference. Soon you will want to make room for even more time in God's Word.

DATE: ....

GOD THINKS YOU'RE AMAZING

Read Zephaniah 3

UNDERSTAND

Zephaniah 3:17 is one of those verses that calms anxious hearts. It offers so much comfort because it tells you some very important things about God. You're reminded that He is with you, that He battles on your behalf, that your very being pleases Him, and that He doesn't keep track of the things you've done wrong in the past.

Know anyone on earth like this? Probably not.

While your friends and family love you and think you're pretty cool, remember that God loves you even more. No one here can come close to feeling the way He does about you. He's a protective, caring, compassionate, and forgiving Father, and He is just crazy about you!

How does it make you feel, knowing the way God thinks about you? Is it easy to believe and accept, or do you struggle to feel worthy of His love and attention? Regardless of how you may feel, God will never change the way He feels, because He created you in His image. And God thinks you're amazing.

....

....

....

....

....

....

....

APPLY

What part of Zephaniah 3:17 encourages your heart the most right now?

What might it look like for God to rejoice over you with joyful songs?

PRAY

DATE: ....

BE THE VOICE OF REASON

Read Genesis 37

UNDERSTAND

Joseph's brothers were so jealous of him. In frustration, they plotted his demise. But Reuben tried to be the voice of reason. Unfortunately, his best efforts failed and his brothers didn't listen.

Your job is not to make others do the right thing. Honestly, you don't have that kind of power over anyone. You can't force others to listen to your wisdom, but you can stand up for what you know is right and speak truth to your friends and family anyway.

God has given you the ability to know right from wrong. And His Holy Spirit in you will guide you as you make choices. It may be scary to stand up and speak out when you feel prompted. Sometimes being the voice of reason isn't popular. But have you considered that maybe God put you in that very situation, with those friends, because He wanted you to help them make the right decision?

....

....

....

....

....

....

....

....

....

APPLY

What role does the Holy Spirit's voice play when you're faced with tough choices?

Do you consider yourself a role model? Why or why not?

PRAY

DATE: ....

ARE YOU ALL IN?

Read Deuteronomy 6:1–19

UNDERSTAND

Think about what it means to love God with all of your heart. . .to love Him with all of your being. . .and to love Him with every bit of strength you have. It may be easier to replace the word *all* with the words *some* or *most*, because *all* is a tall order. It requires everything you've got, and that's hard to give.

Why do you think God commands so much from you? Why doesn't He want to settle for a piece of your heart, a smidge of your being, and a little bit of your strength? Maybe it's because He designed you and knows the beauty of what you have to offer. Maybe it's because God created you to be in a relationship with Him. Or maybe it's a mixture of both.

The one who knows you inside and out wants to be at the top of your list of priorities. He wants you to be all in.

....

....

....

....

....

....

....

....

....

APPLY

What does it mean to love God with all your heart, being, and strength?

What scares you about choosing to be all in with God?

PRAY

DATE: ....

BURNING BUSH MOMENTS

Read Exodus 3

UNDERSTAND

Do you ever pray and ask God to put a huge lighted billboard in your path to show you the way to go? Sometimes we all want His answers to be obnoxiously evident because we're confused on what's the next right step for us. And because we don't want to miss it, we cry out for our own burning bush moment.

The truth is that God doesn't hide the path He's chosen for you. While He may not reveal every detail, He will always show you the next right step. The Word clearly says that if you seek Him, you will find Him. He doesn't play mind games or give you confusing hints to decode. He simply says that when you need answers. . .ask. He will make them recognizable.

It's okay, however, to remind God that Moses needed a big sign. It's okay to ask God to make His answers to your prayers super obvious. He loves you and created you to be in a relationship with Him. That means when you talk to your Father in heaven, He's deeply delighted! So, where do you need His help right now?

....

....

....

....

....

....

....

APPLY

How does God speak to you?

When did you feel God leading you in a certain direction?

PRAY

DATE: ....

WHEN YOU FEEL UNQUALIFIED

Read Exodus 4:1-17

UNDERSTAND

Feeling unqualified is something everyone struggles with from time to time. You're not alone if you lack the confidence and courage to follow God's leading in your life. It often takes His supernatural strength to be able to trust enough to say yes. Maybe God included stories like Moses' to remind you that He didn't make a mistake commissioning you for the job.

Remember that God doesn't call the qualified; He qualifies the called. In other words, if He chooses you for the task, God will give you what you need to walk it out. That doesn't mean it will be easy (or horrible, either). But it's assurance that you will have the tools and skills and wisdom when you need them.

Where is God asking you to step out in faith? Where is He asking you to have epic courage? What situations are requiring you to trust Him more than your circumstances?

....

....

....

....

....

....

....

....

Have you ever felt like you didn't have what it takes to do what God is asking?

What could happen if you decided to say yes to God's calling?

PRAY

DATE: ....

THE CHOICE TO BELIEVE

Read Genesis 15

UNDERSTAND

Abram had to make a choice. Would he choose to believe what God told him, even though it must have seemed almost impossible? Or would Abram let that nasty seed of doubt keep him from trusting God's promise? He chose to believe, and it made him right with God.

You live in a world so full of broken promises that it's almost impossible to believe what you're told, isn't it? Keeping your word isn't a high priority in today's society, and it has taught us that vows are easily broken and unreliable.

But that's not God's way. When He promises something, He never takes it back. He will not let you down. He won't forget about you. God intends to make good on His promise in His perfect time. And when you decide to hold on to that vow no matter what, it deeply delights His heart because He knows the effort it takes.

....

....

....

....

....

....

....

....

....

APPLY

When you're afraid, how do you hold on to God's promises?

Who have you seen trust God no matter what?

PRAY

DATE: ....

DO IT ANYWAY

Read Genesis 6:8–22

UNDERSTAND

What a sad state of the world for God to be so frustrated that His plan for redemption was to destroy every living thing on it. In all the earth, Noah was the only person who pleased Him. This righteous man stood his moral ground even though everyone else—literally every other human being—was ruled by their sinful nature.

Do you think today's society is that different from the one in Noah's time? It doesn't take a rocket scientist to see the mess we are in morally. But that only sets the stage for you to shine God even brighter into the darkness of the world. It shouldn't depress you. Instead, it should make you more resolved to be a modern-day Noah who lives according to God's beautiful plan.

It may not be the popular way to live, but do it anyway. Not because you are better than others but because you know that it matters to God.

....

....

....

....

....

....

....

....

APPLY

What keeps you from saying yes when God asks you to step out of your comfort zone?

How might it feel to be commissioned by God for a specific purpose?

PRAY

DATE: ....

WHEN YOUR SPIRIT IS SPARKED INTO ACTION

Read Haggai 1

UNDERSTAND

Sometimes you need God to intervene and spark you into action. You need Him to get you off the couch, change your mindset, give you enthusiasm, infuse you with courage, or ignite excitement to do something new. With everything on your busy calendar—school, practice, work, friends, family time—you sometimes need an extra push to find the gumption to move forward.

Just like He did for those in Haggai's day, He will for you too: "So the LORD sparked the enthusiasm. . .of the whole remnant of God's people. They began to work on the house of their God" (Haggai 1:14).

Have you ever been too overwhelmed to consider taking something else on or had your heart set on a lazy weekend to watch Netflix? Maybe you've been afraid to try that thing again because it didn't go so well the first time. Or maybe something seems too difficult and you don't want to risk failing.

Ask God to get you moving! Ask Him for courage, perseverance, or time. Sometimes the very thing you need is the Spirit to spark you into action.

....

....

....

....

APPLY

Can you remember a time God sparked you into action?

Where do you need enthusiasm to take the next right step?

PRAY

DATE: ....

YOU MAKE A DIFFERENCE

Read Genesis 39

UNDERSTAND

Did you notice that the Lord blessed *because of* Joseph? God's favor was on him, and Potiphar's home benefitted while Joseph worked there. Even when Joseph was thrown into jail, the Lord's favor was on him and the warden trusted his leadership. Everywhere he went, God was with him, and it made a difference.

God's presence is with you too. Be it a classroom, club meeting, team practice, band concert, job, or place you volunteer, your presence blesses others because of God in you.

It's not about your pride; it's about your faith. When you spend time in the Word and in prayer, when you trust God and follow His path for you, your faith becomes strong. And because you're willing to let God be God, you give Him room to mold you into a beautiful Jesus girl. You become wise, compassionate, and courageous. . .and that blesses others.

....

....

....

....

....

....

....

....

APPLY

As a Jesus girl, how does it make you feel knowing that God's favor is on you?

God working through you can encourage others. Who can you comfort right now?

PRAY

DATE: ....

THE BIG PICTURE

Read Genesis 45

UNDERSTAND

Seeing his brothers again opened Joseph's eyes. He wasn't bitter that they'd disliked him nor angry that they sold him. Joseph didn't blame them. Instead, God blessed him with the big picture.

It's easy to get stuck in situations that feel unbearable. You're distraught for being dumped by that guy or cut from the team. You're frustrated for not getting the lead in the musical or that summer job. And sometimes, it's easy to get mad at God because you've prayed for these things and they still didn't happen.

But what if you decided to trust that God is in control and that if He wanted you to date the boy, make the team, get the lead, or be hired for that job. . .it would've happened? What if you asked God for the big-picture perspective, thanking Him for always knowing what's best?

APPLY

Why is it so hard to see the big picture when you're in the middle of a mess?

....

....

....

....

....

....

....

....

....

....

....

....

How would your perspective change if you trusted that God isn't done yet?

....

....

....

....

....

....

....

....

....

....

....

....

PRAY

....

....

....

....

....

....

DATE: ....

WAITING AND WATCHING FOR GOD

Read Exodus 14:13–31

UNDERSTAND

Exodus 14:14 is often a hard verse to obey, wouldn't you agree? It's not easy to keep your mouth shut when you feel wronged. And staying calm may even be harder. When someone hurts you, lashing out in anger is a more natural reaction to the hurt you're feeling. But God says to let Him handle it.

If you're quick to defend yourself or have the last word, you've taken that initial opportunity away from God to fight for you. And chances are your quick reaction only added fuel to the fire anyway.

What would it take for you to step back and let God battle instead? According to Moses, it would take calmness and quietness. This isn't taking away your voice or suggesting what you think and feel doesn't matter. Tell God everything—get all the hurt and anger out—and then watch and wait as He fights for you.

....

....

....

....

....

....

....

....

APPLY

Is it hard for you to remain calm when you hit rocky times? Why or why not?

What does it mean to you that the Lord will fight for you?

PRAY

DATE: ....

THE TRAP OF LYING

Read Genesis 4:1–15

UNDERSTAND

Cain thought he could get away with murder. When he planned it out in his head, it must have left him with a false sense of security that he would get away with it. But soon after, God confronted him. And when God asked Cain about his brother, He already knew what had been done. Cain miscalculated his plan and his God.

It's easy to lie, especially when you think doing so will save you from getting caught. The problem is that developing that habit and lying on the regular becomes a way of life. Dishonesty no longer bothers you and you lie without worrying about consequences.

Sure, there are little white lies that don't seem to really matter, but they matter to God. And the more you get comfortable with those, the easier it is to move on to the bigger lies.

Choose to be an honest young woman. Be a champion for truth.

....

....

....

....

....

....

....

....

....

APPLY

How has dishonesty caught up with you and resulted in painful consequences?

Are you in the habit of confessing your sins to others and God?

PRAY

DATE: ....

DON'T COMPLAIN. . .TRUST

Read Exodus 16:1–18

UNDERSTAND

The Israelites were quick to forget the miracles, signs, and wonders they'd just witnessed at the hands of God. Over and over they saw God take care of their every need. They watched as Pharaoh finally released them from slavery. They saw the sea part as they walked the dry ground to the other side. They saw it all yet found reason to complain anyway.

Have you ever forgotten the times God showed up for you? Do you sometimes worry if He'll fix that relationship, bring new friends, heal the disease, give you courage, help you forgive, or show you the answer? And does that worry ever come out as anger with a hint of drama?

The next time you want to complain instead of trust, take a breath. Then remind yourself of the times God has been there for you, and thank Him.

....

....

....

....

....

....

....

....

APPLY

Are you a complainer? What keeps you from being content?

....
....
....
....
....
....
....
....
....
....
....
....

How would your life be better if you were satisfied rather than always hungry for more?

....
....
....
....
....
....
....
....
....
....
....

PRAY

....
....
....
....
....
....

DATE: ....

BUILT FOR COMMUNITY

Read Exodus 17:8–16

UNDERSTAND

What a beautiful picture of friends helping friends. All the pressure for the win was on Moses and his ability to keep his arms raised in the air. Arms held high, the army was winning. But when his arms began to lower from exhaustion, the opposing army had the upper hand. Thankfully, Hur and Aaron stood on either side of Moses and held up his arms when he couldn't any longer.

Aren't you glad God knew how much we needed friends? Think through your last week and those times a friend said kind words, bought you ice cream, helped you process hurtful words, gave you a ride, let you borrow a favorite shirt, or invited you to her party. Those friends are gifts from God, here to bless you.

Are you being a good friend back? Are you available to support others when they need help? Remember, God has blessed others with your friendship too.

....

....

....

....

....

....

....

....

APPLY

Think of all the ways friendships bless you. How does your friendship bless others?

Who might need your support and encouragement right now?

PRAY

DATE: ....

MAKING YOUR WAY BACK TO GOD

Read Zechariah 1

UNDERSTAND

In today's scripture reading, God's message was clear: "Come back to Me because I'll be here waiting!" God promises throughout His Word that He will never leave you. So, the truth is that if you're feeling distant from God right now, He's not the one who walked away or turned His back on you.

Maybe life has gotten busy with chores, school, work, practice, friends, or a new hobby. Maybe your family has been traveling or you're in the throes of moving. Life will always be busy and you'll always have a to-do list, and unless making time for God is a priority, it will negatively affect your relationship with Him.

Can you imagine going a week without talking to your bestie? Or not seeing your parents for a month? Or missing two games with your teammates? Distance with those we love and care about is hard!

If you're far from God right now, make your way back to Him in those ways you've connected with Him before. He's waiting!

....

....

....

....

....

....

....

How is your relationship with God right now?

What things do you do that help you feel closest to God?

PRAY

DATE: ....

YOU CAN'T CONTROL OTHERS

Read Exodus 5:17–6:9

UNDERSTAND

The Israelites were understandably cranky. They'd been in slavery for so long. And when Moses told Pharaoh to free them, his request instead made conditions tougher. In their eyes, this man sent to end their bondage didn't make things better; he made them worse. No wonder they didn't want to listen to what he had to say.

Remember, Moses wasn't there to win a popularity contest or shame others into listening to him. God didn't send him to make sure he was heard and believed. Instead, his only job was to speak on behalf of God and then watch Him soften or harden their hearts into action or inaction. Moses didn't have the power to control their responses. His job was to speak.

Release yourself from the expectation that you're doing God's job. Instead, choose to share truths laid on your heart and trust God to do the rest.

APPLY

How do you respond when people don't listen?

You can't control others. How does this free you?

PRAY

DATE: ....

HARD WORK PAYS OFF

Read Genesis 29:15–30

UNDERSTAND

After seven years of work, Jacob didn't receive Rachel's hand in marriage; he ended up with her older sister, Leah. The story is full of twists and turns, but Jacob had to work another seven years to earn Rachel's hand. He had to be joyful and focused rather than frustrated and flippant.

It's easy to finish the project when you know the teacher will give you a good grade. It's easy to run miles at practice knowing you'll start the game. But it takes grit and integrity to give your best when you're not sure your efforts will pay off.

God created you to work. There are things He knew only you could do because of the awesomeness inside you. So when you whine and complain or give anything less than your best effort, you're missing out. What's more, those around you won't get the benefit from what you can bring to the situation or project.

....

....

....

....

....

....

....

....

APPLY

Have you ever worked hard for something and found joy in the effort?

How can you be joyful even if the outcome isn't glamorous or is unexpected?

PRAY

DATE: ....

WHAT DO YOU WORSHIP?

Read Exodus 20

UNDERSTAND

God doesn't mince words when He says there should be *no other gods*. He rightly deserves your devotion and praise. And while you may not worship other gods like Buddha or Allah, it's easier than you might think to place everyday things and much-loved people above Him.

Who or what gets your time? Netflix? Friends? Music? Working out? Parties? Books? Sports or theater? Work? When you let any of these things become more important than God, you're actually putting them higher on your priority list than Him. They become godlike because you focus your time on them more than anything else. And too often, that means God gets what's left over.

Make sure that you find ways to connect with God throughout your day. Talk to Him about what frustrates you. Thank Him for helping and guiding you. Tell Him you love and appreciate who He is in your life. Share your hurt feelings and hopeful expectations. When you do, you're actively letting God know that there is no other god above Him.

....

....

....

....

....

....

APPLY

What are the things you worship?

What are some practical ways you can spend time with God throughout your day?

PRAY

DATE: ....

THE PROBLEM WITH IMPATIENCE

Read Exodus 32:1–24

UNDERSTAND

Moses took a little more time on the mountain than the Israelites thought was necessary, leaving them aggravated. Instead of trusting their leader and their God, they became annoyed and irritated. They got bored. And scripture tells us they complained to Aaron and talked him into making a *replacement* god.

How many times have you found yourself overanxious as you wait for God to show up? Especially when desperate, it's normal to want to grab the reins of control or put your trust in something or someone else. But too often your desire for instant answers leads to unhealthy alternatives that leave you empty.

What's the hardest part about waiting on God? Do you worry He'll forget to respond or not show up altogether? Ask God to grow your trust of Him so you can be patient as you wait for His help. Learn to let God be God, having faith in His timing and His will for your life.

....

....

....

....

....

....

....

APPLY

Are you a patient person? What is the value in learning to be patient?

What are the consequences if you're not patient?

PRAY

DATE: ....

ATTENTION TO DETAIL

Read Genesis 1

UNDERSTAND

Details matter to God. This first chapter in the book of Genesis offers a glimpse into His thought process. These thirty-one verses allow us a peek into the mind of God, giving us the opportunity to see His attention to detail.

He thought of everything. God lit up the darkness and populated the sky with stars; He created the moon and sun so seasons and days would exist. He broke up the water with land and created vegetation for beauty and as a food source. He designed birds to soar in the sky and fish to swim in the oceans. He created the regal lion and the animated monkey and every kind of animal in between. God thought of everything!

Maybe He included these details as an encouragement to you. Think about it. If God can manage every part of creation, can't you trust that He's able to manage every part of your life too?

....

....

....

....

....

....

....

....

APPLY

What part of the creation story intrigues you the most?

What has God created in your life?

PRAY

DATE: ....

THE POWER OF PRAYER

Read Ezra 9

UNDERSTAND

Ezra prayed a desperate prayer that day. He knew that God's people had messed up again, and he wanted to help make things right. Ezra knew this was something only God could fix, and so he cried out for His forgiveness and help.

What an awesome example. This prophet reminds you that so often God is your only hope. And while it's easy to try to remedy the situation yourself, inviting God into the mix is a smart move because He has the power to make things right again.

Whether it's a friendship struggle, a family feud, a class schedule, a team dynamic, a work issue, a hard confession, or anything else you face in life. . .there's power in prayer because God is on the other side of it listening to everything and already making a way for you.

Talk to God and invite Him into your situation. Thank Him, confess, and ask for what you need. He's all ears.

....

....

....

....

....

....

....

....

What role does prayer play in your life?

Do you think there is a right way or a wrong way to pray? Why or why not?

PRAY

DATE: ....

ARMED AND READY

Read Nehemiah 4

UNDERSTAND

The opposition was so great against Nehemiah and the Israelites. They were committed to restoring the wall surrounding Jerusalem, but their enemies had every intention of shutting the project down. Instead of giving in to fear, Nehemiah told the Israelites to work with one hand and to hold a weapon with the other.

This is great advice. The truth is that the enemy of your soul wants to stop you from walking out the plan God has for you and your life. He wants to intimidate you, scare you, and overwhelm you. But you get to choose if his tactics work or not.

There are plenty of weapons available to you, like God's Word, prayer, and community. All of these things can help you stay the course, empowering and encouraging you to keep moving forward.

Whenever God builds, the enemy tries to destroy. Expect opposition when you say yes to God, but don't give in to it. Grab your weapons and do the next right thing.

....

....

....

....

....

....

....

What scriptures comfort you when life gets hard?

What friends and family listen, offer sound advice, and walk the hard path with you?

PRAY

DATE: ....

JUST LOVE EVERYONE

Read Matthew 3

UNDERSTAND

For all intents and purposes, John the Baptist was a little wackadoo. He dressed differently than others. His diet of bugs wasn't considered the norm of the time (or any time, right?). He was eccentric, and there's no doubt people found him to be weird. But none of that disqualified him in God's eyes, because it was God who created the ins and outs of him.

John was fully accepted by God.

Every single one of us battles the urge to judge others in a negative light. It's easy to look at their differences and decide they are unlikable. So often, it's those unique qualities that open people up to being bullied. And that is not cool.

Be someone who celebrates differences. Teach others to respect that we each have qualities worthy of appreciation. And never let yourself join in the crowd when they're making fun of someone.

....

....

....

....

....

....

....

....

APPLY

Why do you think people judge others for being unique?

What are some distinctive things about your friends that you love?

PRAY

DATE: ....

WHERE TRUE DISCERNMENT COMES FROM

Read 1 Kings 3:1-15

UNDERSTAND

We all need good judgment so we can live our best life. We need to be able to see right from wrong, looking past the obvious and into a deeper understanding of situations. Being a Jesus girl means you choose to live with strong morals and a character that reflect the Lord's heart.

But honestly, this is almost impossible without God's help.

We're limited by our human condition. We aren't anywhere close to perfect, and even our best-laid plans to live right can take a sharp left turn into bad decisions and choices—often before we even realize it. Our heart may be in the right place, but even then, we don't always have the ability to make the best judgment call.

But you know what? God promises to give you discernment when you need it. It's something you can ask Him for every single day. It is a heavenly gift that allows you to see the details of a challenging situation clearly—and helps you determine the right next step.

....

....

....

....

....

....

....

APPLY

Have you asked God to show you right from wrong in a confusing situation?

If no, what kept you from asking? If yes, how did it help you navigate the situation?

PRAY

DATE: ....

THE PAIN OF CONSEQUENCES

Read Genesis 3

UNDERSTAND

Their lives changed that day. Adam and Eve directly disobeyed God, giving in to lies from the enemy. In his crafty way, he made them doubt God's goodness. He made Eve feel she was missing out on something. He swayed them into violating the one rule God set for them in the garden. And the consequences were brutal.

Some people believe that God is mean. But the truth is that He doesn't want you to ruin your life or do things that will make you unhappy. God created commands to keep you safe. They are in place because He loves you! At times, it may be hard to embrace them because they feel stuffy or restricting, but you can trust that God has them in place for your protection.

Where are you struggling to make the right choice? What makes it challenging to follow God no matter what? Ask Him for strength and wisdom to follow Him even when disobeying feels easier and more fun.

....

....

....

....

....

....

....

APPLY

How have you seen God use natural consequences to teach you a better way?

Have you asked Jesus to be Lord of your life? How and when?

PRAY

DATE: ....

BE A VOICE OF ENCOURAGEMENT

Read 1 Thessalonians 5

UNDERSTAND

In a world where people can be mean for sport, choose to be someone who is generous with her encouragement. Everyone is quick to tell you everything you're doing wrong and what you need to fix or change. With all that negativity floating around, sometimes a kind word can make all the difference in a friend's day.

Maybe the new kid needs an invitation to sit with you at lunch, or your teacher needs a note that tells her how much she's appreciated. Maybe your server at the restaurant needs to know they did a good job, or the store cashier needs a thank-you. Chances are Mom could use an *I love you*, and complimenting your grandmother's hairdo would make her smile. Everyone needs encouragement.

So decide to be a cheerleader, always on the lookout for opportunities to inspire and motivate those around you every day. It may be exactly what someone needs!

....

....

....

....

....

....

....

What kinds of affirmation do you need to hear the most?

Is there someone who could really use your encouragement today?

PRAY

DATE: ....

YOU ARE MORE THAN YOUR LOOKS

Read Esther 1

UNDERSTAND

The queen refused to go before the king and his guests. She knew they'd been partying, and the thought of showing up made her feel vulnerable. She may have been tired of people only noticing her looks without seeing the depth of her heart. Vashti may have been scared for her safety, unsure what her husband would have required of her.

So rather than risk it, she said. . .no.

The world may tell you that it's all about how you look. It may place importance on your body instead of your brains. Society may say you have to possess beauty to be loved or accepted.

But that is not what God says.

Don't believe the lie that you're deemed valuable based on your looks. Everyone is beautiful in their own way—inside and outside. And never forget that your immeasurable value comes from being a daughter of the most high King—period.

....

....

....

....

....

....

....

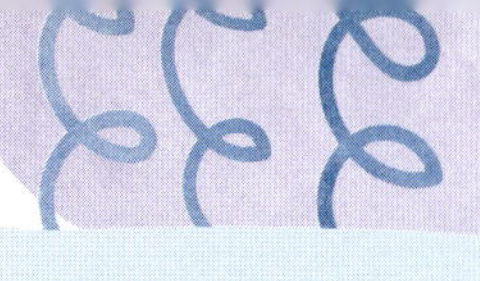

APPLY

Do you pressure yourself to be beautiful? Why or why not?

How does God see you and describe you?

PRAY

DATE: ....

HE CAME FOR YOU

Read Mark 2:1-17

UNDERSTAND

Mark 2:17 is good news for us! Jesus was saying that He chose to step down from His heavenly throne, wrap Himself in human flesh, all so He could offer hope to anyone who had sin in their lives. And at last check, that's everyone, right?

Sometimes we think we have to clean ourselves up and get our act together before we can reach out to God. We're ashamed of our past or our current season of sinning, and so we hide away rather than develop a relationship with Him.

You don't have to have perfect grades or be on the varsity team. You don't have to have a perfect track record of good choices or be a flawless Christian. Being part of the popular crowd at school or having the best summer job in town doesn't matter. Jesus came to earth because He loved you!

Tell God those things that keep you from accepting His unconditional love, and then ask Him to give you the courage and confidence to embrace it! When Jesus said He came to earth for you, He meant exactly that. You were worth the trip from heaven!

....

....

....

....

....

....

Do you consider yourself healthy or sick?

Do you think you have to be flawless or blameless to have a relationship with Jesus?

PRAY

DATE:..

THOSE DARK DAYS

Read Psalm 23

UNDERSTAND

Psalm 23:4 is one of the most quoted verses because it helps us find strength that God is there and we will be okay. The reality is that we will have those dark days whether we want them or not. And it's this reminder that helps us stay strong and trust God through them.

Are you there now?

Are you battling fear over a friendship, feeling abandoned or rejected? Maybe the class or job ended up being harder than expected and you're facing some potentially difficult consequences. Maybe there's a health concern for you, or your parents are considering a divorce. Those are the kind of things that force us to walk through the valley of deepest darkness.

But remember, God is right there with you.

He will bring comfort. He will give direction. And He will never leave your side—not for one second. His love will cast out fear and fill you with peace.

Trust Him to walk you through those dark days.

....

....

....

....

....

....

....

APPLY

When struggles come, do you hold on to God, or do you freak out?

When you felt the closest to God, what was going on in your life?

PRAY

DATE: ....

PROTECT YOURSELF FROM EVIL

Read Exodus 12:1–31

UNDERSTAND

The death of the firstborn was the final plague set to sweep through the land of Egypt. Moses and Aaron had followed God's orders, asking Pharaoh to free the Israelites. But up till now the royal had snubbed his nose at their request despite all the chaos God had brought their way.

In the previous plagues, God had spared the Israelites from them all. In this final one, however, God required their participation.

What a great reminder that sometimes God keeps you tucked away from evil. You may not even know all He has saved you from. But there are other times God asks you to make a choice. He is expecting you to protect yourself from bad influences, dangerous situations, blatant sin, and beliefs that don't align with His truth.

Where is God asking you to stand your ground? What is He asking you to protect yourself from? Where is He requiring your participation?

....

....

....

....

....

....

....

APPLY

What are some ways to protect yourself so you don't follow bad influences?

Why did God require the Israelites to put blood on their doorframes?

PRAY

DATE: ....

YOU ARE WHO YOU HANG OUT WITH

Read 2 Thessalonians 3

UNDERSTAND

You are who you hang out with, which can be super awesome or not good at all. It's very common for a friend's idiosyncrasies, catchphrases, interests, likes and dislikes, manners, thought patterns, and focuses to rub off on you. That's why it's so important to make sure you choose your friends wisely.

What's more, make sure that you're a good influence on others too! How you live your life speaks loudly and has the power to encourage your friends to be their best selves.

Be a focused student. Treat others with kindness. Don't gossip or bully. Live out your faith. Extend grace and forgive. Hold to your morals. Respect authority. Honor your parents. Be nice to your siblings. Make wise choices. Don't let fear rule you. Be a good sport.

Make sure you're the kind of person who calls their friends to a higher standard, and make an intentional decision to be around people who do the same for you.

....

....

....

....

....

....

....

APPLY

Do your friends influence you positively or negatively?

What kind of influence are you on those you hang out with?

PRAY

DATE: ....

GOD KNOWS YOUR NEEDS

Read Genesis 2

UNDERSTAND

God breathed into the nostrils of Adam and it gave him life. He literally needed God's breath to come alive. God was the one who knew exactly what Adam needed in that moment. And as time went on—maybe even before Adam was aware on his own—God recognized another need. Adam needed a partner.

God sees you. He knows exactly what your situations and circumstances require. He is fully aware of what troubles your heart and confuses your mind. God knows what you long for and what scares you. And in His sovereignty, God knows the exact moment you'll need His help.

Today, think about the places you need God's intervention. Tell Him what you're facing and where you're struggling. Let God know every part of your life that feels incomplete. It's not that He doesn't already know those places, but God loves when you share your heart with Him in prayer.

....

....

....

....

....

....

....

APPLY

What are the top three things you desperately need in your life right now?

Do you see God moving in those places yet? How?

PRAY

DATE: ....

STOP TRYING TO BE GOD

Read Psalm 46

UNDERSTAND

The psalmist is being very bold, telling us to be still and know that God is God—to stop working so hard to make everything okay. That means we can surrender our worries, stop talking about them, refuse to control the situation, and let God work. Quite the tall order! But when we do these things, we'll watch as God brings help and healing where we need it the most.

Where is the hardest place to trust God in your life?

Is it in your plans for the future? Maybe in your fears and anxieties about relationships? Maybe in being willing to forgive someone and move on? Maybe in a tough situation with a parent, coach, boss, or teacher? It's natural to want to try to fix your life yourself. You are very capable! But what if you gave God the reins and let go of the control? What if you decided to let God be God. . .and you be you?

....

....

....

....

....

....

....

....

....

Do you let God be God, or do you try to be god by manipulating situations and people?

How would your life look different if you gave God full control?

PRAY

DATE: ....

NO MATTER WHAT

Read Daniel 3

UNDERSTAND

These three men are absolute rock stars in the faith. Talk about raw trust in God! They had no idea if they would live or die, but they knew without a doubt that God was full of goodness either way. What a beautiful example of confidence in the Creator.

It's easy to have faith when life is going well. When everything seems to be going your way, trusting God is easy-peasy. But when your foundation is shaken, your security feels threatened, and your future feels unstable, do you still trust Him?

Shadrach, Meshach, and Abednego stood their ground. Will you?

Even when your family is fighting, you're moving across the country, your best friend walks away, you're failing the class, you didn't make the lead in the musical, or you lost a grandparent. . .you can choose to believe that God only allowed the hard now because He would somehow use it for your benefit later.

....

....

....

....

....

....

....

....

Where do you need the resolve of Shadrach, Meshach, and Abednego in your life?

What would need to change to have this kind of faith?

PRAY

DATE: ....

JESUS WAS TEMPTED TOO

Read Luke 4:1–13

UNDERSTAND

We face temptations of all kinds. Just think about what has tried to get your attention this week alone. Maybe it's been a temptation to lie or cheat. Maybe it was to sneak out of your house or deliberately break curfew. It might have been to use bad language or talk back to authority. Or maybe it was to eat the whole box of cookies or watch something inappropriate on TV.

There are no shortages of temptations. There are opportunities galore to make bad choices. Why not talk to Jesus about them?

Since He could withstand—as a human—forty days of temptation on an empty stomach, wouldn't you think He might be someone who could give you strength and wisdom to withstand what you're facing right now?

He knows the world you live in and all the curiosities that come with it. He knows what interests you and what things attract your attention. He knows those lures that make it hard to choose the right path. And if you ask, He will help you overcome them all.

....

....

....

....

....

....

....

APPLY

What are your greatest temptations?

Jesus faced every temptation. How can this truth comfort you in your struggles?

PRAY

DATE: ....

THE POWER OF REMEMBERING

Read Exodus 13:3–16

UNDERSTAND

The Israelites knew that they had to remember the goodness of God so they could pass that truth on to their children and generations to come. They knew the power of sharing their experiences with family and communities. And since they didn't have books or smartphones to store those stories, they relied on word of mouth.

Your story is your testimony. All those times God showed up in your life can serve as powerful encouragement to others going through a hard time. They are reminders to hope and to trust when things look bad. Can you remember a time someone's story gave you the courage to not give up? Or when knowing that someone made it through a similar situation as the one you're in helped to build your confidence?

We all need to remember that God is our helper, provider, and deliverer. We need to remember that He will protect and heal us. Those are powerful truths to cling to when we need them the most.

....

....

....

....

....

....

....

APPLY

What is your favorite memory of God's goodness in your life or in your family?

Why do you think it's important to talk about and remember these things?

PRAY

DATE: ....

GOD KNOWS IT ALL

Read Nahum 1

UNDERSTAND

Nothing escapes God. He sees every bit of your life lived every day; He has complete understanding of everything you're facing; and He recognizes every time you make the hard choice to put your faith in Him. That means when you decide to trust God with your struggles and challenges, He knows it. And when you run to Him in your hurt or frustration, He realizes your brave choice.

Not only does God recognize your faith and understand the ins and outs of what you're walking through, but He will come to your rescue every time. Through Him, everything you need in that situation or season will be available to you.

God is a safe place to share the things that beat you down on the regular. The next time you're in a mess—be it emotionally, physically, or relationally—reach out to God for help and healing. He is good and compassionate, and He will give you strength to get through it.

....

....

....

....

....

....

....

....

APPLY

What keeps you from reaching out to God when life gets hard?

How can you trust Him more to share problems and burdens with Him?

PRAY

DATE: ....

GOD ALREADY KNOWS

Read Jeremiah 29

UNDERSTAND

God already knows what's ahead. Before He created you, He thought up detailed plans specific just to you. He determined what was allowed into your life—experiences necessary to grow you to be more like Christ.

We crave to be known. We want to be understood and loved. We want people to see our quirky, crazy, fun-loving, sometimes dramatic sides and accept us.

Well, guess what. God knows you better than anyone, even better than you know yourself. He smiled as He planned you! He put all those facets in you on purpose! And that means you are fully known and fully loved by your Creator.

What's more, He loved you so much that He planned your entire life to be full of hope, peace, and well-being. That doesn't mean things will be easy or perfect. But if you cling to Him, you will always get to the other side.

....

....

....

....

....

....

....

APPLY

How does the truth of Jeremiah 29:11 affect your ability to trust God?

Have you ever asked God about your future? Why or why not?

PRAY

DATE: ....

GRATEFUL GRATITUDE

Read Joel 2:1-27

UNDERSTAND

God takes care of His children. While it may not look or feel like God is in the mix, He promises to always be present and to straighten your crooked paths. He'll take care of you and meet every one of your needs. Guaranteed.

Here's where it gets hard to stand firm in your faith. You have to trust that God's way is the best way. You have to trust that His timing is perfect. You have to be patient as He works out the details you're not even aware of. You have to have steadfast courage to take the next step and believe that God will open and close doors.

And through it all, the challenge is to sit in gratitude, thanking Him every day for working in your life. . .even though you may not see it yet. God is consistently working in your relationships, your maturity, your family, and your everyday activities. And His plans for you are always good.

....

....

....

....

....

....

....

....

APPLY

Where is God meeting your needs right now? Have you thanked Him for it?

....

....

....

....

....

....

....

....

....

....

....

....

What are the best and most natural ways you connect with, praise, and thank God?

....

....

....

....

....

....

....

....

....

....

....

PRAY

....

....

....

....

....

....

DATE: ....

FRIENDS CHANGE

Read Genesis 11:1–9

UNDERSTAND

God's command was simple: Go all over the earth and multiply. The flood was over, and it was time to repopulate the world with new life. But instead of obeying His command, the group wanted to stay together.

We like our people, don't we? We have our besties and could never imagine being without them. While God created you for that kind of community, sometimes His plan is for you to move on.

There are friendships that may last a lifetime and others that are seasonal. Your job is to listen to God's voice so you can be where He wants you to be. Your friend group changes when you move states or schools. It can look different when you change teams or summer jobs. Friendships can shift when you start choosing different activities or interests. And as much as you may want to hold on, ask God to show you His will for every relationship.

....

....

....

....

....

....

....

....

APPLY

How has your group of friends changed or stayed the same?

....

....

....

....

....

....

....

....

....

....

....

....

Why do you think God puts new friendships in our lives?

....

....

....

....

....

....

....

....

....

....

....

....

PRAY

....

....

....

....

....

....

DATE: ....

SOMETIMES WE NEED A TIME-OUT

Read Jonah 1

UNDERSTAND

This prophet had a divine time-out. God needed Jonah to take a step back and rethink the path he was on because it was in the opposite direction from God. The Lord had asked him to do something hard—something that scared Jonah—and he tried to run and hide.

Can we agree that so often the things God asks of us are hard? He wants us to accept an apology from someone who really hurt our feelings, invite the new kid to join the group, say no to a party where we know there will be alcohol, or tell the truth when a huge consequence is looming. And if we were honest, we'd admit that the option to run and hide sounds much easier.

God loves you so much that He will sometimes put you in a time-out to collect your thoughts. It gives you a chance to think through your choices. And it gives Him time to speak through your circumstances.

....

....

....

....

....

....

....

APPLY

Has God ever closed a door to get your attention? Why might He do this?

What was the result of that "time-out"? Did you learn anything specific?

PRAY

DATE: ....

IT ALL BOILS DOWN TO THIS

Read Micah 6

UNDERSTAND

Have you ever read the CliffsNotes for a book? It boils the big takeaways down into bite-size morsels. It cuts to the chase, if you will. Micah 6:8 is just that. It's a quick reminder of how God wants you to live.

Be fair to those around you. Love others well. Be loyal and kind. And focus on God more than yourself. Through the prophet Micah, God is giving you the CliffsNotes of His overall desire for your life. Think about His requirements for a moment. Which of them feels difficult to walk out? Are there any that are overwhelming? Do you consider these commands fair or unreasonable? Are you already living this way, or do you have some work to do?

Here is some good truth. These directives are possible only with God's help. You simply cannot live this way without Him. And what's more, He doesn't expect you to be perfect. But He is looking for you to be purposeful in trying.

....

....

....

....

....

....

....

How has God helped you do something that you couldn't do on your own?

What would God say to someone who struggles with being perfect?

PRAY

DATE: ....

YOUR AGE DOESN'T MATTER

Read 1 Timothy 4:6–16

UNDERSTAND

Don't ever let anyone tell you that your age is a deficit. You may not have lived as much life as those older than you, but you can still be a powerful force for good in the world. You can still be a beacon of hope for your generation. You can still have a voice of influence for the kingdom.

Never apologize for being who God made you to be.

And think about this. He decided that now would be the perfect time on the kingdom calendar for you to be alive. God packed you full of gifts that the world needs at this moment. He placed a call on your life to be walked out right now. You have a mighty purpose!

So be a faithful daughter and friend. . .and be known as a truth teller. Make sure your life is marked with good decisions and choices. Choose purity. And be a lover of people, sharing kindness and compassion at every turn.

....

....

....

....

....

....

....

....

APPLY

How does your age affect how others think about you and your abilities?

Is it possible to be a role model no matter how old you are? Why or why not?

PRAY

DATE: ....

BE A GOOD FRIEND

Read Luke 5:17–26

UNDERSTAND

Talk about good friends! Can you even imagine the time and effort it took for these men to hoist their friend to the roof, create a big enough hole for him to fit through, and then gently lower him into the room and in front of Jesus? Their care for him offers us a beautiful example of what good friends look like.

What part of this story means the most to you? Is it that this disabled man had a group to call his own? Maybe it's that they went above and beyond the call of duty to help him out? Is it that they weren't afraid to cause a commotion to help him? Something else?

God created you for community, which means you have a built-in desire to connect with others. There's something so powerful about being surrounded by people who love you and believe in you.

Decide to make friends who encourage you to be the best you. And be that kind of friend right back.

....

....

....

....

....

....

....

....

APPLY

What are the qualities you like most in your friends?

In what ways do you serve your friends?

PRAY

DATE: ....

THIS IS BIG FAITH

Read Habakkuk 3

UNDERSTAND

When you see the word *yet* in scripture, go back and read the section leading up to it because it will help put things in perspective. In Habakkuk 3:17–18, it lets us know that the author was making a conscious decision to hold on to his faith in God regardless of the troubles he saw around him. Rather than give in to feelings of hopelessness, he chose to trust the Lord no matter what.

That's what you call BIG faith. It's when you choose to put on big-girl pants and make those hard decisions to believe God despite your circumstances. It's not letting fear win or insecurities bloom. It's when you keep your eyes focused directly on God and ignore all the mess swirling around you.

How does this encourage you or challenge you?

Where do you need to have BIG faith right now? Ask God to give you the courage and confidence to trust Him with gusto!

....

....

....

....

....

....

....

....

When have you trusted God versus been overwhelmed by circumstances?

How can you use praise to combat fear?

PRAY

DATE: ....

FEAR IS NOT FROM GOD

Read 2 Timothy 1

UNDERSTAND

Second Timothy 1:7 is one of the most power-packed verses in the Bible because it speaks directly about fear. Maybe fear is your constant companion and you don't even realize it controls your choices and decisions. Maybe you're very aware of your fear but don't know how to get past it.

It's important to remember that God will never use fear to punish you or to direct your next step. But the enemy will. As a matter of fact, it's his greatest weapon designed to stop you right in your tracks.

Fear tells you to give up. It says you can't do something so don't even try. It reminds you of all the times you failed and of every embarrassing moment. Fear says you're not good enough, lovable enough, smart enough, wise enough, liked enough, pretty enough, and every other *not enough* you can think of.

But God says you can. You will. You're awesome. And you are enough! So don't let fear run your life anymore.

....

....

....

....

....

....

....

APPLY

If fear doesn't come from God, *where* does it come from? What has it stolen from you?

....

....

....

....

....

....

....

....

....

....

....

....

Do you find it easy or hard to talk to God about your fears? Why?

....

....

....

....

....

....

....

....

....

....

....

....

PRAY

....

....

....

....

....

....

DATE: ....

LET GO AND MOVE ON

Read Hebrews 12

UNDERSTAND

It's common—but not a good strategy—to collect our hurts and carry them around with us. We collect things like mean comments or a friend's betrayal. We collect times we felt rejected or unaccepted by others. We collect failures and fallouts. And sometimes we use them to justify our poor-me mentality, hoping that others will feel sorry for us.

But you know what hoarding them really does? It causes you to lose sight of the awesome plans God created just for you. You get tangled up in all that's bad and wrong, and you stop living with passion and purpose—the very opposite of what God desires for you.

God wants to heal those hurts so you can let go of them. And when you do that, you're supernaturally freed up to run with joy and determination the race He has set before you! It doesn't mean you won't remember those hard, messy times, but they won't have power over you anymore.

....

....

....

....

....

....

....

What is one thing you can do to let go of hurts from your past?

What does it mean to you to have people cheering you on in life and faith?

PRAY

DATE: ....

DON'T HIDE WHO YOU REALLY ARE

Read Genesis 12

UNDERSTAND

Abram was afraid for his life and less concerned for his wife. In that moment, he was more worried about surviving than making sure his marriage was thriving. In his fear, he asked his wife to be someone she was not. How do you think that made her feel?

Can you think of someone who told you that you were not okay? Has there been a voice in your life that's been a constant reminder that you needed to change to be loved or to be accepted? Hear this now: That is not how God feels about you.

You delight your heavenly Father—stumbles, fumbles, and all. He made you *on* purpose and *with* purpose, and His heart for you is so very good. Trust that you were an intentional creation, especially when someone tells you the opposite. And if you need reminding, ask God to do the reminding.

APPLY

Do you believe God created you perfect in His sight? Why or why not?

What three things do you love most about yourself? Tell them to God.

PRAY

DATE: ....

CONSIDER IT JOY?

Read James 1

UNDERSTAND

Have you ever wondered just how you're supposed to live out James 1:2? How is a broken friendship, a failing grade, a losing season, a screaming match, a divorce, a grandparent's death, a school change, or a scary diagnosis an opportunity for joy?

Many agree this is super challenging because it doesn't feel normal or natural to see sad and messy moments as opportunities for anything more than throwing a good ole temper tantrum. Amen? And it's because of that, you have to understand that you'll absolutely need God's help to do it.

On your own, finding this kind of eternal perspective feels hopeless. But in these times, cry out to God and ask Him to increase your faith so you can trust His plans. Ask Him to comfort you and bring peace.

And don't forget to ask God to restore your joy—not joy that bad things happened, but joy that He will get you through it.

....

....

....

....

....

....

....

APPLY

What difficult thing in the past can you look back at and see that it was helpful?

In the moment, do you tend to lean on God, or do you ever give in to despair? Why?

PRAY

DATE: ....

THIS IS WHO YOU REALLY ARE

Read 1 Peter 2:1–10

UNDERSTAND

Who does the world say that you are? Chances are you hear plenty of messages full of *not good enough* and *if only* comments, leaving you to doubt your lovability. And sometimes, those messages can be so loud!

But you know what else? We can often be the ones whispering lies of worthlessness to our own selves. Sometimes we're our worst critic. God must have known the tendency we'd have to beat ourselves up, so He made sure to include scriptures reminding us who we really are.

Take a moment to let this sink in: You are chosen, you are royalty, you are special, and you are God's. When He created you, He filled your heart with love and your mind with wisdom. He made you with gifts and talents like no one else, and you have God's stamp of approval.

That means you don't need it from anyone else. You are 100 percent loved and accepted because you are His.

....

....

....

....

....

....

....

Do you allow negative self-talk? What are the mean-spirited messages you tell yourself?

How do you think God sees you? What does the Bible say?

PRAY

DATE: ....

NO ONE IS PERFECT

Read 1 John 1

UNDERSTAND

Somewhere along the way, we decided that being honest about our mess-ups was a bad thing. We became scared to admit failures or flubs and instead wanted to present ourselves as perfect to those around us.

Maybe we're afraid of being judged or ridiculed by others. Maybe we think that our lovability is based on our performance. Maybe we're so insecure, certain that our flaws only confirm the lie we're believing that says we're not good enough. Or maybe we have unrealistic expectations for ourselves—ones we can't possibly live up to.

But guess what. God isn't expecting you to be perfect. Jesus is—and will always be—the only unflawed person to walk on planet earth. Instead, God wants you to live with purpose and passion. He wants you to try, knowing you'll fail at times. He wants you to live the adventure without being worried that you're defective or damaged.

So, don't hide your human condition. It's okay to not be perfect, because no one is.

....

....

....

....

....

....

APPLY

Is it hard for you to admit it when you are wrong or have done something wrong?

Do you think God expects you to be flawless? Why or why not?

PRAY

DATE: ....

STAND UP FOR OTHERS

Read Luke 23:13–43

UNDERSTAND

Jesus was hanging on the cross, dying. He had been betrayed by Judas and denied by Peter, and now the religious leaders were mocking Him publicly. No one boldly faced His accusers and stood up for Him. Those supporting Him were few and far between. Think how lonely Jesus must have felt in that moment.

Think about your own life. Have you ever felt as if no one was in your corner? Maybe some mean girls or jeering boys were focusing in on you and nobody was around to help. Maybe you were bullied for your faith or morals, and you were left standing alone.

Or maybe you were the one to mock someone else.

Decide today that you will stand up for those targeted by bullies. Surround yourself with friends who won't tolerate the mocking of others. Be someone willing to stand up for kindness and respect at all costs. And know that with Jesus' help, you can do it.

APPLY

If you've ever been mocked or bullied, what did you learn from that experience?

....

....

....

....

....

....

....

....

....

....

....

....

Why do you think certain people make fun of others?

....

....

....

....

....

....

....

....

....

....

....

....

PRAY

....

....

....

....

....

....

DATE: ....

WE'VE ALL SINNED AND FALLEN SHORT

Read John 8:1-30

UNDERSTAND

Have you ever looked at your mess-ups and decided they're not as bad as another person's mess-ups? It's easy to look at someone else's sins and think you're better than them. You may decide you're smarter, holier, nicer, wiser, or more worthy of love. You may think, *Well at least I didn't do* that*!* Maybe your sin is hidden while their sin is public, so it naturally makes you look like your life is all together.

The temptation is to ignore the parts of your heart and life you need to work on, justifying your sin. But that's not God's hope for you.

The Bible says there is no condemnation in Christ. Admitting your sin doesn't make you bad or unlovable. It makes you right with God. It removes any barrier in your relationship with Him so you can live your best life together.

Before pointing your finger at others, ask God to help you see your own struggles. And ask God for compassion, realizing everyone makes mistakes.

APPLY

Do you think some sins are worse than others? Why or why not?

How can you be more authentic and vulnerable in your relationships?

PRAY

DATE: ....

KEEP YOUR EYES OPEN

Read Jude

UNDERSTAND

Influencers are everywhere (and we're not just talking about that girl on social media who swears by some product or brand). But despite influencers being everywhere, we shouldn't let ourselves be influenced by everyone. Most of us know this already; we're usually quick to notice when someone says something or does something that's *miles* apart from what we believe is good and right. The trouble is it's harder to see when it's an ever-so-slight deviation from truth.

It may be a simple encouragement to cheat on a test or sneak out for the party. It could be a suggestion to tell a little lie to your parents or play innocent rather than admit fault and accept the natural consequences. These small tweaks in how you live can often seem like no big deal, but they matter to God.

So be aware of whose advice you take. Be conscious of whose suggestions you follow. Make sure your decisions line up with what God wants for you. Ask yourself, *Would this make Him happy?* If the answer is no, walk away knowing He'll honor your desire to do right.

....

....

....

....

....

....

....

Have you ever done something just because of peer pressure?

How can you guard yourself from negative peer pressure?

PRAY

DATE: ....

THE POWER OF YOUR STORY

Read Revelation 12

UNDERSTAND

This may be a challenging book and chapter to read and understand, but one thing is crystal clear: The blood Jesus spilled on the cross for your salvation plus your story of how He has shown up in your life is a powerful combination.

Stories are compelling motivators that help remind you that you can trust your heavenly Father with whatever you're facing right now. Doesn't it comfort you to know that others have walked a similar path as you—and survived? These accounts grow hope that you'll be okay in the end and that everything will work out one way or another.

Can you remember a time you were encouraged to take a leap of faith because you heard someone talk about their own? Or inspired by a friend's testimony that she was finally able to overcome her insecurities by choosing to believe what God said about her instead of listening to others?

Stories carry weight. Listen to them and share them whenever you need a reminder of God's goodness.

....

....

....

....

....

....

What are some stories you've heard that deeply encouraged you?

What are the common themes of these stories?

PRAY

DATE: ....

FIGHT FOR THOSE YOU LOVE

Read Genesis 14:1–16

UNDERSTAND

Did you notice that as soon as Abram heard that his nephew was in trouble, he acted? He didn't ignore it. He didn't put it at the end of his to-do list or think that his time was too valuable or that he had better things to do. Instead, Abram immediately gathered his finest men and went after Lot.

Investing in the lives of others is messy business. But God created you to be in community with others. He knows we each need a tribe of people to come alongside us as we walk out our one and only life. And so often He uses others to be His hands and feet, helping us through tough times.

Who needs you right now? Who is God putting on your heart to help? Go fight for them. If you ask, God will give you exactly what you need to do it.

APPLY

How can you help the people you love when they are struggling?

What can you do now for someone who needs an ally in their battle?

PRAY

DATE: ....

ANCHOR YOUR HOPE IN GOD

Read Isaiah 40:12–31

UNDERSTAND

We all need hope. It's the most powerful motivator, and without it we fall into deep despair. Hope is what makes us try again or take a risk. It's what gives us the strength to put on our big-girl pants and move forward. Hope is necessary to living with purpose.

God must have known the value of hope, because He established Himself as hope itself. He promises that if you will have confidence in His power in your life—trusting Him with everything—you will benefit in huge ways! Anchoring your hope in God will give you strength, courage, motivation, and energy to never give up.

Where do you place your hope? Sometimes it's in people or processes. It could be in your own strength or a favorable horoscope. Hope could rest in past successes or a good-luck charm. But none of these have the real lasting power to encourage your heart with confidence and bravery. Only faith in God can do that.

....

....

....

....

....

....

....

....

APPLY

When you're tired and weary, what are the things you do to reclaim your energy?

How might a quick prayer asking God for confidence help in tough moments?

PRAY

DATE: ....

MODEL THE GOOD

Read 3 John

UNDERSTAND

Whether you realize it or not, your life preaches. The words you use, the things you do, how you respond to the ups and downs of life—all are watched by others. And when they know you are a Jesus girl, your responses tell those around you about God.

How do you react when you get benched or when the teacher calls you out in front of the class? When your friend group dumps you or tells your secrets to others, how do you respond? When your parents are known as the "strict" parents or your sibling isn't liked at school, how do you handle it?

Make no mistake, your actions preach. But don't think you have to be perfect, because that kind of pressure just sets you up for failure. Instead, God is asking you to be mindful, aware that you have an amazing opportunity to point others to Him with your life.

Whenever possible, choose to model the good.

APPLY

What helps you stay true to your beliefs when others are pressuring you?

....

....

....

....

....

....

....

....

....

....

....

....

Who are the people you look up to? What do you like about them?

....

....

....

....

....

....

....

....

....

....

....

....

PRAY

....

....

....

....

....

....

DATE: ....

DON'T BE ASHAMED TO SHARE JESUS

Read Romans 1

UNDERSTAND

It can be terrifying to share your faith with others. Part of it may be that you're shy or feel uncomfortable talking in a group, but it could also be scary because telling others about your belief in Jesus is a vulnerable act.

And vulnerability can sometimes feel unsafe.

What's more, the world often seems hostile to the idea of following God. Finding the courage to open up and expose your faith may feel like being a seal in shark-infested waters. And it's that fear of rejection that convinces you to keep your mouth shut and your faith hidden.

But don't let fear or insecurity keep you in hiding. You're part of God's plan A to share Him with the world. He's counting on your words and actions to point others to Him. And in those times when you need the courage to speak up, He will give it to you when you ask. Guaranteed.

....

....

....

....

....

....

....

APPLY

How do you feel about sharing your own testimony?

If your friends or classmates were asked if you're a Christian, what would they say?

PRAY

DATE: ....

LISTEN BEFORE YOU SPEAK

Read Proverbs 18

UNDERSTAND

One of the kindest things you can do for those you love is let them have a voice. Allowing your friends space to share how they feel or to unpack a bad day tells them you care. It lets them know they're valued. It helps them process life with a trusted friend.

It lets them be heard in a world that is loud and overpowering.

Then once they've been able to talk, ask God for wisdom on how to respond. Do they need advice? Do they need validation? Do they need an apology? Do they need encouragement or perspective? Maybe you need to ask them exactly what they need from you in that moment.

Who are the good listeners in your life? Who are the friends and family who give you room to vent or lament? Who are the safe people who let you open up in honesty and share vulnerably?

Learn from them. Listening is a powerful way to let someone know they matter.

....

....

....

....

....

....

....

APPLY

How can you become a better listener?

Can you remember a time you spoke too soon and made a fool of yourself?

PRAY

DATE: ....

KEEP YOUR EYES ON GOD

Read Acts 7

UNDERSTAND

Stephen's circumstances were not good. He'd been sharing God's story, and it angered a mob, who took him outside the city to stone him. But rather than be overwhelmed by the situation, Stephen leaned on his faith, and he gazed into the heavens and fixed his eyes on God.

What tough circumstances are you facing right now? Maybe you fell out with a friend, are at odds with a parent, aren't seeing eye to eye with a coach, or got fired from a job. These are the kinds of things that can take you out, keeping you sad or angry at the world. They can ruin your day and make you want to hide under your covers.

What if instead, you look past your circumstances and focus on God. Rather than wallow, you pray? Rather than replay the moment over and over again in your mind, you open the Bible? What if you choose to believe God's promises more than any fear created by the mess you're in?

....

....

....

....

....

....

....

....

APPLY

How can you focus on God rather than the scary circumstances you're facing?

If you tend to focus on fear, what would it look like to make a different choice?

PRAY

DATE: ....

HOW YOU LIVE MATTERS

Read 1 Corinthians 10

UNDERSTAND

In 1 Corinthians 10:31, Paul encouraged the church in Corinth to be mindful of how they live. . .because it matters. He reminded them that their goal—and our goal—should be to glorify and honor the Lord with how we live.

Your choices carry weight with your friends. And because you're a Jesus girl, people watch how you live your life. Spreading rumors at school, cheating on tests, sneaking out, lying to parents, ignoring others, using curse words, being mean-spirited, causing drama, and treating adults rudely does nothing to promote the Lord to those around you.

If asked, would your teachers and classmates know that you love the Lord? Would they notice that you are kind and compassionate toward others? Would you be known as a stinker or a person who tries to live the right life? When your peers are in trouble or struggling with something, would you be a safe place?

This isn't a call to be perfect. It's an invitation to live with purpose. Are you up for it?

....

....

....

....

....

....

APPLY

What do you think it means to live in a way that glorifies and honors God?

What would have to change in your words or actions to make this happen?

PRAY

DATE: ....

YOU DON'T HAVE TO FIGURE IT ALL OUT

Read Proverbs 3

UNDERSTAND

How do you trust God from the bottom of your heart? Doing so requires that you choose to believe that God is who He says He is and will do what He says He'll do. It's deciding daily (sometimes hourly) to surrender your thoughts, ideas, and plans; it's making the hard choice to flex your faith muscle.

We're so inclined to try to figure things out on our own. Instead of listening for God's voice, we ask our friends and family for their input. And rather than wait for God to show us the next right step, we follow the path we think is best.

Think about it. What would have to change in your responses to life to make trusting God easier?

Would you have to give yourself a twenty-four-hour time-out before making a move? Ask your friends to pray that God will open and close the right doors? Spend time reading the Bible, waiting for Him to speak?

....

....

....

....

....

....

....

APPLY

How do you hear God's voice best?

What could you change so you could hear His voice better?

PRAY

DATE: ....

STAY OR AWAY: WHAT'S THE BEST CHOICE?

Read Genesis 16

UNDERSTAND

Hagar had it rough. She was put in a lose-lose situation and punished for carrying a child she never wanted to carry. While she may not have had the best attitude, it was no excuse for abuse. It never is. And feeling overwhelmed by all she was enduring, she chose to run away because it seemed the best choice. There was no way for her to win.

Maybe you are feeling the same as Hagar—unloved, unappreciated, unseen. Maybe there are haters in your life who make it almost unbearable to get through the day. Maybe your family is in a tight spot and everyone's bad mood seems to be pointed in your direction. Maybe a friend turned her back on you and is sharing secrets you never meant to be shared.

You have a choice to make. Do you stay and advocate for yourself, or do you walk away in wisdom? This is a God-sized question. Why not ask what He has to say?

....

....

....

....

....

....

....

APPLY

Do you stand up for yourself, or do you run away in an effort to avoid confrontation?

How do you know when it's wiser to fight or walk away?

PRAY

DATE: ....

YOUR PROTECTIVE DADDY

Read Psalm 17

UNDERSTAND

Your heavenly Daddy is terribly protective of you. Anything that comes into your life—the good and the not-so-good—has received His stamp of approval and is allowed only if it will benefit you and glorify Him. He is crazy about you, a proud Father! God wants only the very best for His daughter.

So knowing all that, think about the fact that He is the one who chose your earthly father. How does that make you feel? Because the truth is that sometimes fathers are the bomb diggity, and other times they fall very short of awesome. Sometimes they make us feel loved and special and other times not so much.

Regardless of the flaws of your earthly dad, your heavenly one will never let you down. He will never turn His back. He will never hurt you. And what's more, God will give you the grace and perspective to love your here-and-now dad even in his imperfection.

Is your dad the kind of father who protects you? How?

Only your heavenly Father is perfect. Where can you extend grace to your dad?

PRAY

DATE: ....

WHO IS GOD TO YOU?

Read 2 Samuel 22

UNDERSTAND

To David, God was his everything. He was true, a stronghold, a place for refuge, a shield, a rescuer, a tower, and his savior from trouble. This king knew his only hope was in the hands of God, and so he decided to trust and believe that the Lord would be who he needed Him to be.

Who is God to you?

Think back to times you've seen Him show up. What were the results? Did He heal you or someone you loved? Did He make a way when it looked like there was no way out? Did God open a door at the right time, or did He close one to protect you? Did He give you courage, wisdom, strength, peace, or perspective when you had none?

David was in the habit of telling God what he thought of Him. It probably encouraged him to remember and delighted God to hear. Spend time telling God exactly who He is to you.

....

....

....

....

....

....

....

....

Who do you run to when you need help navigating tough situations?

How can you make God your go-to in these situations?

PRAY

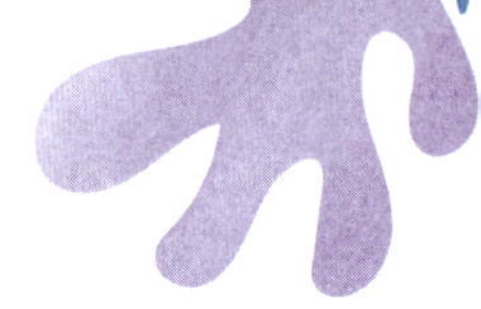

DATE: ....

DRAWING A LINE IN THE SAND

Read 2 Samuel 18:1–18

UNDERSTAND

This unnamed man drew a line in the sand. He decided to obey King David's command to protect his son Absalom. And no matter the temptation to cross the line—even for a ton of silver—he'd set a boundary he was unwilling to compromise.

There will always be lures and cravings that will try to persuade you to cross the lines you've set for yourself. It's hard to stay true to what you know is right because society often has different standards than those of Jesus. What the world says is true and right rarely aligns with what the Bible says. And the pressure to fit in often requires you to cross the boundaries you've put in place.

Ask God to help you stand firm against temptations. Ask Him for the courage to stand your ground even when it may be the unpopular decision. Ask for wisdom and discernment to see when you're getting too close to the line you've drawn in the sand.

APPLY

What's the difference between setting boundaries and building walls?

What are some decisions you can choose before you are faced with them?

PRAY

DATE: ....

IT'S ALL ABOUT PERSPECTIVE

Read 2 Corinthians 4

UNDERSTAND

What an eternal perspective! Paul refused to see any struggle or challenge that came his way in a negative light. Instead, he understood that God had allowed them for a powerful purpose. What about you?

When your boyfriend dumps you or your bestie shares your secret. . . When your parents ground you or the coach cuts you from the team. . . When your boss fires you or you don't get picked for the musical. . . What's your response?

This is where you get to choose how you see a tough situation. You can trust that God allowed it because He'll use it for His glory and your benefit. Or you can go into drama mode, throwing the best pity party in the history of the world.

One way highlights your faith, and the other exposes the lack of it. One way shows an eternal perspective, and the other reveals a worldly, selfish view.

Getting hurt, being scared, and facing a letdown are normal parts of life. But it's what you choose to do with them that matters.

....

....

....

....

....

....

....

APPLY

How do you react in tough, stressful, or hard situations?

Why do you think God allows painful and messy moments?

PRAY

DATE: ....

THE URGE TO COVER IT UP

Read 2 Samuel 11

UNDERSTAND

David made a horrible error in judgment. Not only did he sleep with a woman married to another man, but he then had her husband killed so the truth was kept hidden. What's more, with Uriah out of the picture David could marry Bathsheba.

This king was a hot mess of bad decisions. He could have owned his bad choice and asked for forgiveness. He could have repented and made things right. But David decided that the best plan was to cover up his sin.

Maybe you can understand his choice to hide what he'd done. Chances are you have too.

Sometimes it feels safer to keep our blunders and bloopers hidden so we don't have to suffer the consequences. But God knows everything. And He is ready and willing to forgive your every sin when you confess them to Him.

It's always best to just be honest. No one thinks you're perfect, but you can choose to be honest.

APPLY

When you make a mistake, do you ever try to cover it up? Why or why not?

How would this world be different if everyone chose to be honest?

PRAY

DATE: ....

COURAGEOUS FAITH

Read 1 Samuel 17:26–58

UNDERSTAND

Young David had no room for doubt. Rather than worry, he held steadfastly to his courageous faith. In his bones he knew that God would equip him to defeat Goliath. And so David stepped in and stepped up, and the rest is history.

Where do you need that kind of faith today? What situation or person is challenging you to flex your faith muscle like never before? What circumstances are causing you to be fearful or insecure?

Are you worried a friendship might be over? Are you concerned about a struggle within the family? Are you trying something new or giving up something that you've loved? Are you switching teams or friend groups? Do you feel inadequate for the job you're about to start or unprepared for the semester?

Your courageous faith in God will give you the strength, wisdom, and perseverance you'll need to battle any giant that comes your way!

APPLY

Do you think it's ever risky to trust God to supply everything you need?

What do the words *courageous faith* mean to you?

PRAY

DATE: ....

GOD OF THE IMPOSSIBLE

Read Genesis 17

UNDERSTAND

God had just revealed His epic plan for Abraham and his descendants. In that moment, He made a covenant, promising things that only He could make possible. Abraham was intrigued, excited, and probably in complete awe. And then God shared a promise that made him fall down and laugh. The idea of him fathering a child at the ripe old age of one hundred felt impossible. But not to God.

How about you? Has God whispered things that feel overwhelming and unrealistic? Maybe it's to speak up or speak out about hard things. Maybe He's promised something that doesn't seem possible because of bad choices you've made. Or maybe you feel unqualified to follow the path He has laid out for you.

Let God be God. He specializes in the impossible. He can do anything, fix anything, change anything. Your job is to be obedient to do the next right thing.

....

....

....

....

....

....

....

....

APPLY

How do you respond to situations that look impossible?

When have you had to rely on God for an outcome?

PRAY

DATE: ....

DON'T BE AFRAID TO FOLLOW GOD

Read 1 Samuel 10

UNDERSTAND

Saul was hiding. It's funny to think this soon-to-be-named king was so scared of stepping into his God-given role that he tried to hide. The truth is that walking out God's will can be scary and hard and make us feel insecure in our abilities. Have you ever experienced that in life?

Maybe you felt nudged to share Jesus with a friend or your testimony at youth group. Maybe you felt led to go on the mission trip rather than to summer camp with friends. Or maybe you felt God asking you to give money to your church instead of buying new clothes. Sometimes we get scared about what He may be asking or feel inadequate for the job, and so like Saul we try to hide instead of embracing what we believe God is asking.

Think about those fears that keep you stuck, unwilling or unable to follow God's leading. What are you afraid of? Have you told God about it?

....

....

....

....

....

....

....

APPLY

Are you ever tempted to hide from doing what's right? Why or why not?

When have you obeyed God even though it was super hard? What was the result?

PRAY

DATE: ....

THE CONSTANT BULLY

Read 1 Samuel 17:1–25

UNDERSTAND

The Philistine was a giant named Goliath, and he was an epic fighter with huge muscles, proper training, and top-of-the-line weapons. There is no doubt he was a force to be reckoned with. And every day for forty days, he stood before the Israelite army bullying them with his words. King Saul and his men were scared because they forgot how powerful their God was.

You have bullies too—situations and people that freak you out. It could be a health concern or a rude teammate. You may bully yourself with thoughts of inadequacy about the big class presentation in a few weeks. Maybe there are mean girls who are making your school year miserable. Yes, we will all face giants in our lives, which is why we can't forget that our powerful and faithful Father is stronger!

Never forget that He is always with you and always for you. And when you need His help, ask Him to defeat the giants that constantly taunt you.

....

....

....

....

....

....

....

APPLY

What are some of the giants you're facing today? How do you respond to them?

How does this well-known Bible story encourage you today?

PRAY

DATE: ....

BE FRUITY!

Read Galatians 5

UNDERSTAND

Being a Jesus girl has benefits. One of them is being gifted with the fruits of the Spirit. These gifts are cultivated in you through the Holy Spirit's supervision, and these fruits are meant to benefit not only you. . .but others as well. These take time to grow to maturity—just as all good things do—but you can access them when you need them now.

Sometimes we think we're fully responsible for mustering up these gifts ourselves. We place the burden on us to make these a part of our everyday lives. But we are not God. And when we struggle to have joy, have lost our peace, are short on patience and kindness, can't grab on to faith, and have abandoned love and gentleness toward others, we feel like failures.

Be careful to not set unrealistic expectations for yourself. You're not the gardener. But you can practice using these fruits in your friendships right now. And when you find one that needs to mature more, ask God to help!

APPLY

Which fruits of the Spirit do you see in your life right now?

....

....

....

....

....

....

....

....

....

....

....

....

Which fruits do you need the Holy Spirit to grow in you?

....

....

....

....

....

....

....

....

....

....

....

....

PRAY

....

....

....

....

....

....

DATE: ....

CHOOSING TO BE KIND

Read 1 Samuel 1:1–20

UNDERSTAND

As if Hannah didn't have enough to trouble her already, she had to deal with her rival's taunts year after year after year. Maybe Hannah wanted to strike back—it would have been tempting, right?—but instead, she sought God's help. Sometimes turning the other cheek is challenging; obeying God's command to love even our enemies is hard, really hard. But it's a choice we have to make. We can be nice or we can be mean. The choice is ours.

God wants you to be kind. That doesn't mean you're a doormat that everyone gets to walk all over. That doesn't mean you have to let others bully or make fun of you. And it certainly doesn't mean you are weak or unworthy of love.

It just means that you take your faith seriously.

It means you're letting God work in the situation.

It means you're choosing not to treat difficult people the way they've treated you.

Instead of stooping to their level, ask God for wisdom and for Him to intervene. Ask a trusted adult for help. Advocating for yourself is a powerful skill. It's choosing to be kind to yourself.

....

....

....

....

....

APPLY

Why do you think certain people choose to be mean to others?

Since God commands us to love others, is it possible to justify treating anyone cruelly?

PRAY

DATE: ....

LONGING FOR THE WRONG THINGS

Read Genesis 19:23–29

UNDERSTAND

And just like that, Lot's wife turned into a pillar of salt. Many argue that looking back was her way of innocently remembering what she was leaving behind. But God was clear in His directive to not turn around. Their life in the city of Sodom was nothing to miss. He was saving them, and turning back toward the city was disobedience.

Part of trusting God is trusting His reasoning. You don't always get to know the why—at least not this side of heaven. He says in His Word that His plans for you are always good plans. So when God is clear, telling you what to do or what not to do, you can (and you should) confidently trust Him.

God's heart for you is always good!

What is God asking you to leave behind? What makes doing so difficult? And how can you choose faith over your fleshly desires so you can stay in God's will?

....

....

....

....

....

....

....

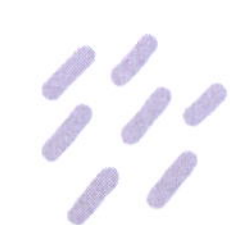

APPLY

What things, places, or relationships do you miss?

How do you know when you should let go of something or when it's worth fighting for?

PRAY

DATE: ....

CHOOSE TO BE LOYAL AND FAITHFUL

Read Ruth 1

UNDERSTAND

Ruth was a rock star. When she decided to stay with Naomi, she knew it could end her chances to remarry and have a family. But love for her mother-in-law trumped her own desires. More than anything else, Ruth wanted to be loyal and faithful to Naomi.

It's hard to look past our own desires and focus instead on someone else's. Because our default button is to look out for number one, choosing to put someone's needs ahead of our own is a big deal. What's more, God sees and will bless it.

As Ruth's story goes on, she ends up meeting Boaz, getting married, and having a son named Obed. He later became King David's grandfather, placing Ruth in the direct lineage of Jesus.

God saw and blessed Ruth's loyalty. And He will also bless you for being selfless and faithful to those you love.

....

....

....

....

....

....

....

....

APPLY

What was Ruth giving up when she chose to stay with her mother-in-law?

Who are your faithful friends? What does their friendship mean to you?

PRAY

DATE:..

BE TRUSTWORTHY

Read Judges 16:4–22

UNDERSTAND

Delilah was digging for information to hurt Samson. She may have acted like she cared for him, but she didn't. She made a deal with the Philistines, agreeing to exchange Samson's secret for a bunch of silver. And once he shared that confidential information with her, it was the beginning of the end for Samson.

When someone chooses to open up to you, it's important you choose to be a trustworthy friend. Maybe your friend is struggling with their parents' divorce and wants to talk, is being left out of the group and feels unwanted, or needs advice on how to handle a rude teammate. If they are willing to open up, decide to be a safe friend.

Can you identify the loyal and faithful friends in your life? And can you also identify those who are not? Be smart with your heart, and be reliable to those who share theirs with you.

Who are the family members and friends you can trust with your heart?

Have you ever been betrayed by a friend? Are you still friends?

PRAY

DATE: ....

THE LIES WE BELIEVE

Read Judges 6:11–24

UNDERSTAND

Every day you're bombarded with lies—hurtful untruths about who you are. From rude comments, to perfect images on social media, to high expectations from others, to your own bullying thoughts, it's easy to let truth become clouded by lies. Every day you have a choice to make: Will you adopt those lies as your truth, or will you believe you are who God says you are?

You may ask, *What does God really think about me?* That's a fair question and an important one. Because if you're to choose to believe Him over the lies, you have to know that His heart for you is good, right?

That's where God's Word comes into play in your life. In its pages, God talks to you. It's where He reveals who He is and where He reminds you of who you were created to be. The Bible is a powerful weapon to help battle hurtful lies. Make time to read it every single day.

....

....

....

....

....

....

....

APPLY

Do you see the good, or do you focus only on things you don't like about yourself? Why?

How does Gideon's story encourage you?

PRAY

DATE: ....

ARMOR UP!

Read Ephesians 6:10-20

UNDERSTAND

In today's reading, Paul told us that our struggles really aren't with people. Of course, people can make us mad and hurt our feelings, but he went on to say that the true battle we face is with the enemy. He and his minions are behind the evil we see in the world.

Because you are so loved, God created a set of divine armor that you can access. The belt of truth, the breastplate of righteousness, the gospel of peace as shoes, the shield of faith, the helmet of salvation, and the sword of the Spirit are designed to protect you against the schemes of the devil.

Don't be afraid of him, and don't focus your energy on him either. The enemy is not worth your time. But do be aware that he's working behind the scenes to discourage you at every turn. And know that God has already taken care of that. His armor will give you the edge over the devil every time.

....

....

....

....

....

....

....

....

APPLY

Which piece of the armor of God stood out to you the most?

Why do you think it's important to armor up?

PRAY

DATE: ....

GOD-GIVEN GIRL POWER

Read Judges 4

UNDERSTAND

Jael killed a man in such a gory way. The details of that story may be hard to stomach, but like Deborah in that same chapter, she chose to obey God. The point of the story isn't that murdering is acceptable. It is not. The point is that God often chooses women for hard tasks. He values everyone equally, and in His mind and heart, girls are just as awesome as boys.

Maybe God included their stories in His Word so that you would know that you have immeasurable value to the one who created you. God doesn't measure worth by your sex, skin color, age, or anything else. Instead, He is looking for the faithful ones willing to step up and step out for Him.

Warrior, God equipped you with a huge dose of girl power, and He is hoping you will choose to use it to further the kingdom.

APPLY

Do you ever feel that you're less than because you're a girl? Why or why not?

How are strong women in the Bible alike? How do their stories encourage you?

PRAY

DATE: ....

GO AHEAD, ASK FOR THE IMPOSSIBLE

Read Joshua 10:1–14

UNDERSTAND

Can you even imagine a crazier request than for the sun to literally stop in the sky? Joshua knew that he needed the sunlight so he could defeat his enemies, and so he boldly asked the Lord to stop the earth from rotating on its axis.

Joshua wasn't afraid to ask for something that seemed impossible. Are you? Where do you need God's help but are afraid to ask for it? Do you think God is incapable or unwilling?

Maybe your parents are divorcing and you want them to reconcile. Maybe a cross-country move is planned but you want to stay put. Maybe you want to be friends with a certain group of girls but can't find a way to connect.

Be bold like Joshua in your requests to God. He may not always say yes, but He will always listen and answer in the way that's best for you.

....

....

....

....

....

....

....

What keeps you from asking bold prayers?

Why do you think God chose to include this story from Joshua's life in His Word?

PRAY

DATE: ....

WHAT'S FIRST IN YOUR LIFE?

Read Genesis 22:1–18

UNDERSTAND

God asked Abraham to do something unbelievably difficult. He asked him to sacrifice the child He had promised to him and Sarah. Isaac was a miracle baby on so many levels, and it's not hard to imagine the gut punch such a request would pack. But because God was first in Abraham's life, this man of God stepped out in obedience without question.

Think about it for a second. Where does your relationship with God rank in your life? When you consider friends and school, family and sports, and everything in between, where does God fit in? Does He get your attention every day, or is He easily replaceable? Do you think God feels like a high priority on your calendar?

Take inventory of your priorities and find ways to connect with God in meaningful ways every day. It matters. How can you make Him feel first in your life?

....

....

....

....

....

....

....

....

APPLY

Is God first in your life? What do your actions and words reveal as most important?

....

....

....

....

....

....

....

....

....

....

....

....

How do you respond when God asks very hard things of you?

....

....

....

....

....

....

....

....

....

....

....

....

PRAY

....

....

....

....

....

....

DATE: ....

WHEN YOU'RE WORRIED. . .PRAY!

Read Philippians 4

UNDERSTAND

What's the antidote to worry? Prayer. Do you realize how very powerful prayer can be as a weapon in your arsenal?

What is your usual response to anxiety? Do you talk to your friends about it? Journal it out? Tell a trusted family member? Go into meltdown mode? Respond in anger, lashing out at those you love? Stress eat? Hide in bed? Chances are you have lots of different reactions when you're frazzled.

But in the middle of all these options, have you ever just sat down and prayed? Have you ever cried out to God in your pain? Have you shared your fears with Him? Well, guess what. He wants to hear you share every single detail of the situations that stress you out. God is never too busy or too burdened to give you His full attention.

And what's more, He has exactly what you need to navigate through the concerns that weigh heavily on your heart.

....

....

....

....

....

....

....

APPLY

What are the things that worry you the most?

How can you change how you react to the things that cause worry?

PRAY

DATE: ....

FORGIVING FREES YOU

Read Colossians 3:1–17

UNDERSTAND

Sometimes we choose not to forgive because we think doing so lets the other person off the hook for hurting us. We think forgiving means that the pain we felt wasn't real and that the mean-spirited things they did to us—intentionally or not—weren't rude or wrong. But none of that is true. Those are lies that keep us trapped in unforgiveness.

Here's some powerful truth. When you choose to forgive someone, it 100 percent benefits you because holding on to an offense traps you in a prison—one you cannot get out of.

Think about how much time you spent replaying the mean words your friend said to you, or revisiting the hurt you felt for not being invited to the party. Did those moments slowly begin to overtake your thoughts, and the memories hurt you over and over and over again? Holding on to that unforgiveness imprisoned you, whether you knew it or not.

Be quick to forgive. Let it go, and live free!

....

....

....

....

....

....

....

APPLY

What person or situation do you find hard to forgive?

Who do you think benefits most from forgiveness–the forgiver or the forgiven?

PRAY

DATE: ....

YOU BE YOU, LET THEM BE THEM

Read Genesis 27:1-35

UNDERSTAND

Rebekah's decision to have Jacob pretend to be his brother showed a lack of judgment. The message was simple: If you change your appearance, there's a reward on the other side. So Jacob listened to his mother and presented himself as Esau, but it cost him something.

Have you ever thought that if you were different—thinner, smarter, stronger, funnier—you'd be better? Maybe you'd be more popular or be noticed by the cute boys. Maybe you'd get the academic award or be the lead in the musical. Maybe somewhere along the way, you decided who you are right now wasn't enough. So instead of embracing your awesomeness, you created a fake version of yourself, hoping for acceptance.

God made you on purpose. All your quirks and uniqueness. All your nerdiness and coolness. They were all intentional. So be yourself. If God wanted you to be different, you would be. What's more, He delights in you!

....

....

....

....

....

....

....

APPLY

In what ways do you try to fit in rather than be yourself?

What messages are you listening to right now? Are there changes you need to make?

PRAY

CHECK OUT THESE PRAYER MAPS FOR THE ENTIRE FAMILY. . .

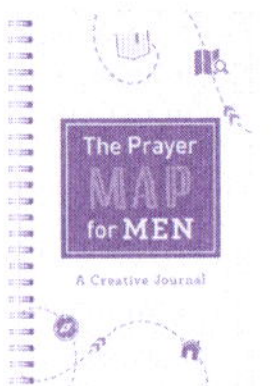

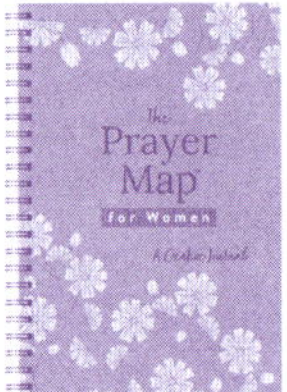

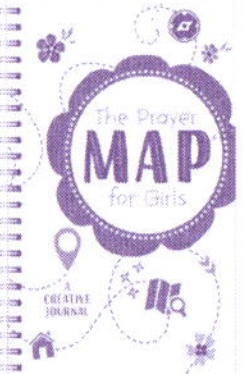

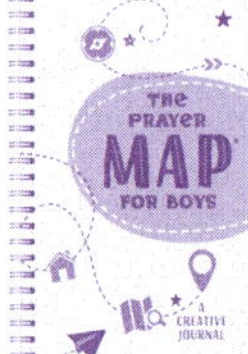

The Prayer Map for Men
978-1-64352-438-2

The Prayer Map for Women
978-1-63609-762-6
978-1-63609-763-3

The Prayer Map for Girls
978-1-68322-559-1

The Prayer Map for Boys
978-1-68322-558-4

The Prayer Map for Teens
978-1-68322-556-0

The Prayer Map for Teen Girls
978-1-63609-803-6

These purposeful prayer journals are a fun and creative way to more fully experience the power of prayer. Each page guides you to write out thoughts, ideas, and lists. . .which then creates a specific "map" for you to follow as you talk to God. Each map includes a spot to record the date, so you can look back on your prayers and see how God has worked in your life. *The Prayer Map* will not only encourage you to spend time talking with God about the things that matter most. . .it will also help you build a healthy spiritual habit of continual prayer for life!

Spiral Bound

Find These and More from Barbour Books at Your Favorite Bookstore or www.barbourbooks.com